CW01475285

Zoom for Beginners

The Top 5 Hidden Features To Master Zoom Meetings For Teachers And Take The Quality Of Your Audio And Video Online Lessons, Webinars, And Live Stream To The Next Level

zoom

MAXINE TARYN

Table of Contents

Introduction

Zoom is a free service that lets you chat using big groups on a mobile device or your personal computer. The difference between others, along with Zoom chat solutions, is the variety of participants. A Zoom assembly can, while Skype could get up to 50 callers in one meeting, have around a million participants, showing up in a grid design to 49 of these. Schools, businesses use meetings to be conducted by Zoom, maintain classes, and host virtual occasions. Another characteristic is that participants do not require perhaps or a Zoom accounts the Zoom program to combine a meeting. While this makes Zoom, bypassing those measures will restrict what you could do.

Security and Privacy Problems

It is vital that before we research Zoom any farther, Zoom claims to possess encryption, meaning that Zoom ought to have the ability to get audio and assembly video. Zoom gets the capacity to get assembly data as they please, but studies have proven differently. This defect could compromise any information that is transmitted via the service. Zoom has information privacy issues. By way of instance, it's been captured

1

sharing consumer information without the consumer's knowledge with firms like Facebook. Also, it keeps files, cloud records, and messages. For groups and businesses with vouchers, these subscriptions' administrators have an amazing amount of power over their workers' accounts. They track their Zoom information or could combine any worker's assembly. The concern is known as zoo bombing. It is where users attempt to interrupt them by revealing offensive material. Zoom's founders added security upgrades, like requiring assembly passwords to fight such trolls. Because of these issues, several organizations have prohibited using Zoom. You can have an experience so long as you take precautions.

Setting up Zoom

To begin, visit Zoom.us if you are using a computer or get the program employing an Android or iOS device.

In the opening screen, click on subscribe for free to make a free account. You may sign up having an email address, or together with Facebook account or your Google. When you confirm your accounts and finish the program, Zoom will download the program. Follow the prompts.

It's somewhat, although Zoom's version is free to use. Your meetings will be limited to twenty-five minutes. Once 40 minutes are up, it is possible to remake or rejoin the assembly immediately. You could even buy a subscription that eliminates those limits and adds additional attributes, such as innovative meeting controls and cloud storage of your video files.

Combining a Meeting

There are methods by inputting to combine a Zoom assembly—a Meeting ID, together with your internet browser, or clicking on an invitation connection. You may use whichever method works best for you personally.

- To combine with the Meeting ID:

- In the Zoom main display, click on Join.

- Enter the Meeting ID and click on Join.

- Input the password, and then click Join Meeting.

- You will be asked if you would like to connect with or without a video. Select Join with Video.

- Before you go into space, you might be put from the Waiting Room first. Until the server permits you to combine, if that's the case, you're remaining here.

To combine with an invitation connection:

A different means is via an invitation connection. Zoom will inquire if you would like the program to shoot over when you click on a Zoom connection. Select available Zoom, and you're going to go through the procedure of connecting the assembly. You might have to give Zoom consent to use the microphone and your camera, especially when this is the very first meeting.

The Way to Better Protect Your Meetings

You need to, although Zoom goals to be user friendly, simply take a few precautions. Let's discuss a couple of configurations and features that may help maintain your Zoom expertise orderly and secure.

- **Waiting Room**: Whenever a person attempts to combine a meeting, then they are placed at the Waiting Room by default. They won't be able to put in the meeting before the server approves them. It restrains the flow of participants and could enable you to filter out guests. You can disable or enable the Waiting Room by selecting Permit Waiting Room and clicking Safety.

- **Gallery View**: When lots of men and women are in one assembly, Gallery View can arrange everyone in a grid design. Click Gallery View from the corner to trigger it.

- **Display sharing limitations**: Screen sharing lets a participant exhibit the contents of the display to the full meeting. But guests benefit from the feature. To limit screen sharing, click on the arrow, and select Advanced Sharing Alternatives. Beneath the question, "Who will share?" Select Just Host.

- **Mute a player**: should you have to mute a player, click on the Staff button, then examine the Participants box to the right for the individual of your choice. Hover the title above and choose Mute. It's possible to unmute using the same method.

- **Eliminate undesirable guests**: You're able to kick out a participant off your meeting. Hover above, click the title and Remove. By default, that player will be unable to rejoin the assembly.

- **Lock the assembly**: In case you don't need anyone else to combine your assembly, it is possible to lock it and keep out beginners. Click Security, and then choose Lock Meeting. You can unlock the assembly.

Aside from discussion, Zoom includes several useful Attributes, such as webinars, meeting transcripts, and document sharing. Even though it's nice to use for casual conversations and talks, we advocate not using Zoom for whatever involves sensitive information. Hopefully, Zoom's founders will continue to enhance the stage and strengthen its safety.

Chapter 1: The Basics of Zoom

Which is better between Microsoft Teams and Zoom?

As the UC showcase is moving continuously from UC to UCaaS, the primary serious situation that most clients are bantering with us is no longer Skype for Business versus Cisco, yet the cloud situation (which presently includes both video conferencing and sound, with a beginning (Zoom Phone usefulness) of Zoom versus Microsoft Teams in the cloud, and with regards to contrasting Microsoft Teams versus Zoom, the arrangement is similarly as precarious in the cutting edge UCaaS condition now as it was in the old fight among Microsoft and Cisco.

In the course of the most recent few years, every one of these moderately new stages has seen a quick turn of events, gathering a significant number of highlights and fans. Try not to squint; the progressing rivalry, creation, and satisfaction of new situations for end-client and endeavor satisfaction are probably going to be quick-fire over in any event the following scarcely any years.

Numerous organizations are at present in the Skype for Business blend. In any case, with the ongoing declaration of the finish of-life date for Skype for Business Online (and the hypothesis that the on-prem version would have a comparable destiny), it is provoking numerous IT groups to determine what their subsequent stage will be for their biological system of availability and participation.

So, how would you settle on Zoom and Microsoft Teams? To start with, take a gander at the separate of every stage and afterward jump into comparing them as close as possible to a level playing field.

Zoom

Zoom is a pioneer (and possibly the packs most prominent since its April IPO) in the video correspondences industry, tending to computerized interchanges at all endpoints through their cloud stage for video, sound conferencing, coordinated effort, visiting, and online classes.

How Are Microsoft Teams?

Microsoft Teams is the widely inclusive workstream joint effort with Microsoft in addition to a brought together correspondences stage—interfacing gatherings, calls, visits, and record offer to the Office 365 application stack to unite everybody in a common workspace.

Breakdown of the Microsoft Teams vs. Zoom

Microsoft Teams and Zoom both meet and contend at a significant level by giving a scope of video conferencing devices (counting room frameworks) and UC communication administrations. Boring more top to bottom into the more mind-boggling usefulness, usability, evaluating, and arrangement is the way organizations can decide compromises and settle on the correct choices concerning which stage is the match.

1. *Characteristics*

Where applications are concerned, both Zoom and Teams permit online gatherings, discussions, calls, screen sharing, and document sharing. Microsoft's cooperation of Teams and its Office 365 stage is the distinction between the two. It makes it workable for Microsoft Teams to be a one-stop-look for some associations. It additionally permits consistent, coordinated effort, reinforcements, and the quest for documents. In any case, going some approach to supplement the consolidation of Microsoft's Office365, Zoom and Slack highlights a wide-going relationship and an assortment of innovative blends.

Zoom, as an association, is a much more current association than Microsoft's behemoth. However, it prompts rivaling its forceful guide, and because it does not need to stress over overseeing (and in the end leaving) many inheritance clients at the premises.

2. *UX (Utility Interface)*

In Microsoft Teams versus Zoom banter, the UI and experience are where Zoom exceeds expectations. Zoom clients are, for the most part raving about its straightforward interface and the capacity to get end clients fully operational with restricted to no preparation or IT support.

Microsoft Teams face a greater test as clients need to get to grasp with how to impart in different systems and groups, incorporate document sharing, just as the other Office 365 applications incorporated with groups. Even though the full scope of intuitive workstream highlights incorporated with Teams empowers it to give a more extensive field of utilization and situations (and along these lines a more noteworthy worth) than Zoom, this particular degree is likewise, in specific regards, its Achilles heel as respects on board.

3. Room Systems

At the point when territories of the field Zoom versus Groups keep on turning out to be exceptionally commoditized, one field of remarkable qualification is the "space frameworks" that are worked inside an undertaking. A room format can go from a fundamental arrangement of the cluster space to a special meeting space for chiefs. Albeit both give application control, contact redesigns, versatile friend's cooperation, and double screen room support, Zoom has the extra bit of leeway of tallying individuals, and Teams have vicinity discovery. Another differentiation between Zoom and Microsoft Teams is that Zoom confirms all integrators and equipment providers. At the same time, Teams affirm just the equipment arrangements.

4. Pricing

Microsoft Teams and Zoom offer each a free form of the stage, offering further developed highlights with paid plans.

Microsoft Teams Free form incorporates limited visits and coordinated effort, applications, and administrations for profitability, gatherings, and calls, and security. Two enormous pieces that are absent with the free form incorporate organization instruments or backing from Microsoft.

The free form of Zoom incorporates gatherings that can have up to 100 members (with a gathering meeting breaking point of 40 minutes), boundless 1:1 gatherings, online help, video and web conferencing highlights, bunch cooperation highlights, and security.

Microsoft's Premium arrangement is insignificantly less expensive per client than the proportionate Pro arrangement for Zoom. However, they are valued similarly to their corporate plans.

5. UC Telephony

The capacity to make calls at an undertaking level is significant, particularly for video, sound, conferencing, and informing business interchanges. This sort of highlight has been at first a fortress of Microsoft, as Zoom did not have at first a telephone framework item.

The Zoom Telephone is the endeavor voice reaction. The advanced and quickly developing cloud telephone framework offers shrewd call steering and the board, auto-chaperon/IVR, interoperability with common endpoints like voice message, call history, guest ID, and portable dialing, besides to call recording. As with Microsoft Teams, it offers the product on both work areas and cell phones. Besides, Zoom's "Present to Your Own Carrier" framework is an immediate reaction to the Direct Routing capacity of Teams, empowering Zoom Phone associations to utilize built up PSTN specialist co-ops in numerous world markets.

6. Zoom Debate

The greatest success for Microsoft Teams is its tight, prepared in combination with Office 365 applications. In any case, past that, Microsoft Teams have more than 70 mixes that incorporate ticket the board alternatives, surveys, climate, news, and so on.

Incorporations, for the most part, on account of Microsoft, are too placed client information into its system. On the other side, the Zoom is frequently added to different stages as a joining. One extraordinary case of this is how Slack and Zoom work aggregately. Notwithstanding the Slack blend, Zoom has more than 100 mixes, including an Office 365 combination.

Zoom and Teams: If you are thinking about the two frameworks running at the same time, you would require a typical administration system that works for both. It is only that Power Suite does!

In actuality, on the two Teams and Zoom, we are progressively observing huge organizations deciding to "normalize." Microsoft Teams are great for coordinated interior effort. However, Zoom is regularly favored for outer work, with clients or with visitor merchants. Since they speak with each other, it is straightforward for clients to construct explicit situations in which to utilize when.

Multiplatform in the new advanced workforce is turning out to be perpetually the current norm. An examination found in an ongoing overview that 85 percent of clients utilize various stages for shared applications.

Zoom Features

1. Use Snap Camera

It is the desktop category of Snapchat that gives users the power to include several filters to beautify them from the application so that they can build lenses. Users can distribute the lenses with the platform and set it as a default. The attribute is a wonderful one that you will enjoy using, especially if you put together a group call to your relatives or friends.

If you want to utilize it, you need to get its app for the version of your device and select an image utilizing any of the available lenses. After performing that task, launch the app and navigate your way to settings. Beneath the section for video, modify the location of the camera from the menu that drops down to the snap camera feature.

2. Share Your Screen

It is one of the most outstanding attributes of the platform, and everyone can utilize this one. Lots of companies utilize this attribute for remote or online help, while few users share visuals to see an movie or watch something together. You must turn the feature on if you want to utilize it.

To use it, just start a video interaction and select a share screen beneath the page. You can also allow the feature for the active window or the entire visual display. For maximum experience, you should turn on the device sound.

3. Unify Third-Party Applications

The platform has lots of compatibility with third-party apps that you can unify easily with one tap. If you want to participate in meetings through the platform, get the app from the store, and you are good to go. You can also utilize the feature to import the schedules you create for the interaction through outlook or the calendar app from Google.

You can meet relatives and business partners on several platforms and begin interaction with only one click. You should know that you can find an app that can perform that function very well. You can locate every app that you require on the platform store.

4. Allow Records

Another important trick that the platform can perform is recording conversation held by the entire group of people involved in the interaction. For example, you can record the interaction on your gadget by tapping the record control key while the interaction is in progress, and it will begin.

The files of the conversation will be inside the documents section. The platform can also provide recordings via the cloud, but only users of a certain stage can utilize this feature; the paid accounts can enjoy this benefit.

5. Audio Transcript

The platform consists of a important attribute that users can utilize to transcribe the audio recording of a interaction automatically. Users can use it to keep records and important parts of interaction inside a VTT text file. Only paid accounts that want to record via cloud have the opportunity to utilize this attribute.

If you are one of the paid accounts, you should launch the platform browser for recording and allow records for the cloud. Now select advanced settings and tick allow on the audio transcript. Anytime you find yourself in a interaction, select record for cloud beneath the page. The platform will send an email after a few minutes, notifying you of the status of the transcript.

6. Create a Schedule for Interactions

You will find the option to create a interaction schedule on the desktop app of the platform. You need to launch the app, and that can waste an little bit of your time. But if you wish to perform that task quickly, get the scheduler which a free extension for you to use. Get and include an event there.

7. Stealth Mode

It is a wonderful attribute associated with the platform. It ensures that users gain access to video interactions with no sound. It is wonderful to utilize when you get access when the interaction is in progress and want to avoid interruption at all cost. It is important to fix your device mic.

8. Launch the App and Select Settings

Tick boxes you wish to include from the audio section to mute the mic anytime you enter a integration beneath the visual display.

You can participate in a interaction without turning your video on, which is important for low bandwidth areas and location with quality problems.

1. Launch the app and select settings.

2. Tick the turn video off anytime you want to participate in a interaction.

3. To toggle on the mic, tap the control key beneath the visual display while the conversation is on.

4. Emoji on screen.

If the host of a interaction mutes your account, you can display your reaction with the utilization of emoji. You can decide which to send, and there are lots of available options, including the clapping and thumbs up. It is easy to communicate your feelings with it.

Whenever you want to use in and interaction, select reactions beneath the visual conversation display, and select your desired choice. It can disappear in less than ten seconds. If the interaction admin allows the non-verbal response attribute, attendants can put an logo like raising an finger, which indicates that they want to contribute to the interaction. Each individual in the group can see the emoji replies.

9. Accommodate Above One Hundred People

You can put together more than one hundred people together in one meeting, which is a wonderful advantage for schools and business organizations. But you need a paid account to enjoy that advantage.

If you subscribe to the premium package, you can invite and accommodate at least one thousand attendants. It is also a wonderful advantage for remote and online workers because they can utilize the platform to communicate with co-workers as well as relatives.

10. Zoom Paid Plans

The platform is free for everyone to utilize; you can even use it without signing up. However, you must know that the platform comes with different plans. The basic plan gives access to an limited number of minutes for the interaction, which is forty minutes.

If you go for the pro plan, it provides a twenty-four-hour limit, which you can consider a lot of time if that is what you require to complete your project. You can also utilize the platform to run your organization even if you do not have wireless.

The platform lets every user host video interactions with at least one hundred people multiple times. The pro plan offers at least one gigabyte of cloud storage for your recording activities, a increased time duration for the interaction, and improved add-ons. It is also a important feature for large companies because of the number of people it can accommodate.

Chapter 2: How to Use Zoom

In a free Zoom account, video conferencing for more than 2 participants lasts 40 minutes (a new connection is required every 40 minutes or a new link is generated).

Video conferencing can be organized in two modes:

- Instant Conference mode, in which a new access link is created each time (predefined option)

- Using a personal conference identifier (PMI). The mode can be selected by clicking on the button of the drop-down menu to the right of the inscription "New Conference."

For the first time, it is recommended to tick "Use my personal identifier": this setting will allow you to create a permanent link to a video conference. This will facilitate reconnection after 40 minutes (if the duration of the conference is more than 40 minutes), and will also allow students to send the link in advance. In the mode without using a personal identifier, a new link will be created every 40 minutes, which must be sent to students.

To start a conference, click on the "New Conference" button. The conference room will open.

Video Conference Room Menu Buttons:

- "Enter audio conferencing" allows you to conduct audio conferencing.

- "Enable video" allows you to enable/disable the video.

- "Invite" allows you to copy the link and send it to students. After clicking on the "Copy URL" button, the link will be automatically copied to the computer's memory (clipboard), after which you will immediately need to paste it into the letter/message using the "Paste" right mouse button or CTRL + V hot keys. The "Copy Invitation" button allows you to copy the text for an email automatically generated by Zoom.

- "Manage participants" allows you to see everyone who has joined the conference (a window appears on the right or a separate window pops up). In the lower right corner you can set additional settings: mute for all participants in the microphone; sound notification that someone has connected/disconnected from the conference. The ability to rename members is useful for tracking attendance. It is recommended that all participants in the video conference correctly reflect their name and surname, and at the end of the lesson take a photo of the screen in order to mark those who are absent in the journal (if the webinar is not being recorded). To rename, you need to mouse over your name, click on the menu for details and select "Rename."

- "Demonstration of the screen" on the desktop.

- "Chat" allows you to open a window for communication with participants. In the chat, you can write to all students/participants, as well as to someone personally. The chat window allows you to even attach files and send them to the general conversation, however, the sent files are not displayed on mobile versions (on smartphones and tablets).

- "Recording" allows you to record conferences so that you can play them back later.

- "Reaction" allows you to send emoticons.

Zoom allows you to demonstrate the screen on a computer, tablet and mobile devices with the installed Zoom application. In order to enable the screen demonstration, you need to click on the button "Screen Demo" located on the conference toolbar. You can choose a separate application that is already open on your computer, desktop, message board.

After starting the screen demonstration, the conference controls are moved to the menu, which you can drag to any point on the screen:

- Turn on/off the sound: Turn on or off your microphone.

- Start/stop video: Turn on or stop your video in the conference.

- Participants/manage participants: View or manage participants (if you are a organizer).

New demo: Start a new screen demonstration. You will again be asked to select a screen for a demonstration.

- Pause Demo: Pause your current screencast.

- Comment: Use screen sharing tools to draw, add text, etc.

- Details: Hover over a item to call up additional parameters.

Zoom allows you to demonstrate the screen of your computer—this is convenient if you want to show students how to work in some specific program. (It is important to remember that the demonstration of the entire screen will display all the file names, applications on your desktop). For such a demonstration, click "Screen Demo"—Desktop/Desktop 1.

Also, the screen demonstration allows you to run a marker board ("Message Board"), on which both the teacher and students can write. In the settings, you can choose whether students can show their screens/files or not (for example, when protecting projects, students can be given the opportunity to broadcast and switch slides on their own). By default, Zoom is set to "Demonstration can be performed by one participant at a time." In order for the student to be able to demonstrate his screen, you need to stop your own screen demonstration by clicking on "Stop sharing" on the control panel. Only after that another participant will be able to start the broadcast.

During the screen broadcast, you, as well as other conference participants, can comment on the slides using the additional "Comment" tool (ie draw, circle, tick). When you click on the "Comment" button, an additional menu will appear. This feature is useful for highlighting something on a slide. You (as the organizer of the conference) can delete (delete using the Eraser tool) all notes and comments. Participants are only those entries that they themselves have applied. To exit this function, click on the cross in the upper left corner of the additional panel.

Sometimes, recording a whole videoconference is required for work. There are two functions for this:

- Immediately after the start of the video conference, click on three points on the control panel and select "Record."

- Set automatic recording in the settings panel.

You Choose Your Own Storage Location in the Settings Menu

In the selected folder for each webinar Zoom creates a separate folder with files and date/time. Zoom also records video conferencing audio files separately. It can be used for podcast or audio lecture. The file is stored in the same folder as the webinar itself.

In order to divide students into subgroups (session rooms), you must check them in the "Advanced Settings."

After clicking on the "Show More Settings" button, Zoom will open a browser page with advanced account settings. The first time you log in through the browser, you will need to re-authorize (entering your username and password). After authorization, in the window that opens, click on the inscription "At the conference (advanced)" and enable the option "Session rooms."

After activating the "Session Halls" from the next conference, they will be available in the menu. To configure session rooms, click on the "Details" -> Session Halls button. Set the number of halls (subgroups), type Separation of participants (automatic or manual). After that, click on the Create Session Halls button.

Halls can be renamed (for example, by the name of subgroups or mini-projects), you can add halls (subgroups), as well as manually redistribute participants. When everything is ready, click "Open all the halls."

Each student will be invited to enter the session room and must accept the invitation. Those who do not accept the invitation will remain in the main conference. After the students disperse into the session rooms, they will be able to hear and interact only with those who are with them in a particular room. In this case, the chat will be available to everyone.

In order to complete the group work in the session rooms, you need to click on the button "Close all rooms" in the menu of session rooms. The group will have exactly 60 seconds left to complete the work, after which everyone will automatically be returned to the general conference.

To end the video conference, click the End Conference button. You can:

- End the conference: the video conference ends, the recording stops, all participants leave the video conference.

- Leave the conference: in this case, students/colleagues may remain to discuss something.

Chapter 3: Advanced Tips and Tricks to Get the Most Out of Zoom

Start a New Meeting

If you are hosting a meeting, click on the 'New Meeting' option which is represented by the orange icon. You will enter an interface that enables you to change the settings according to your preferences.

Audio Settings

First, you will tweak the audio settings. To begin with, find the 'Join Audio' at the bottom-left corner of the window and click the arrow beside it. Click on 'Audio Settings' from the dropdown menu.

You can always access this window by clicking on the setting icon on the top right part of the screen.

- Once the window pops up, click on the dropdown list located on the right side of 'Test Speaker' and select the speaker you prefer. You can either choose your headphone jack, your device's speaker, or any other speaker that is linked externally. We would recommend that you wear headphones as it will block out background noise and keep your meeting private if other people are around.

- Next, you should check the microphone quality. Click on the dropdown menu on the right side of 'Test Mic.' Depending on the microphone device you are using, select the appropriate option. If you have an external microphone connected to your system, the list will display the name. If not, select 'the same as the system' to use the device's microphone.

- Then, you will check the input level of your microphone and voice quality. Start talking and view the slider besides 'Input Level' as it transitions from red to green. Your audio is stable if you are in the green zone (not too slow and not too loud). Check the box beside 'Automatically adjust microphone volume' to make it easier.

- Leave the other settings as they are. You can probably check the box that says 'Join audio by computer when joining a meeting' to access the same setup as soon as you join a call.

Video Settings

Now, we will tweak the video settings. Click on 'Video' located above 'Audio' in the left panel.

- As soon as you click on 'Video,' a box appears with a message saying, 'Zoom would like to access the camera.' Click on 'OK.' The black box in this picture will display what is seen by your front-facing camera. It is how the other participants will see you during the call. You can adjust your position and device to provide a clear view.

- If you have other devices or webcams attached externally to your video interface, select the device from the dropdown menu beside 'Camera.' Leave the other settings as they are, and exit the box.

Stop Video Option

Once your audio and video settings are in place, you are good to go. Close the setting page and click on the button "New Meeting" to start a meeting. If you need the call to be just audio, you can select the 'Stop Video' option on the bottom-left corner of the window, as you access to the meeting.

Invite New Participants

The next step will involve inviting participants to the call. Select the 'Participants' option on the bottom panel of the window and then click on "Invite."

You can either invite people from your contact list or via email. The easiest way is to click on 'Copy URL' and send the generated meeting URL with the people you wish to invite. Exit the box. Once you send this URL to the preferred participants, they can easily access the meeting by pasting this URL in their browser. You can also text or send the meeting password to your participants to join the discussion.

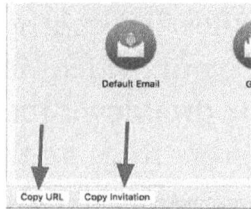

Manage Participants

We will now manage the participants that have permission to access the meeting. Click on 'Participants' on the bottom panel of the main window.

- If you move your mouse over the participants' names, you can mute a particular participant or mute all of them by selecting 'Mute All' at the bottom. This functionality is extremely useful when a single person needs speaking or is instructing everyone.

Chat Options

Access the 'Chat' option on the bottom of the main window. It will open a popup window. It will allow you to write comments and send messages during the meeting. You can also upload files or photos from your device, Google Drive, or Dropbox by clicking on the file icon.

It is particularly convenient if you want to discuss certain specifications during the meeting, such as presentations, reports, or diagrams. In case you wish to send a private message to a participant, you will need to click on "everyone" and select from the list the person that you wish to contact.

Record a Meeting

To record the meeting, select 'Record' at the bottom of the main window. As soon as you click the option, you will notice a pulsing red icon in the window's top-left corner. This signal shows that the meeting is being recorded. The participants will also be aware of the recording as the red icon will be displayed beside your name in the vertical window on the screen's right side. You can also stop or pause the recording by clicking on the respective buttons beside the recording icon.

To access the recording and choose a particular location to save the recorded data, select 'zoom.us' on the top panel of your window and go to 'Preferences.'

Next, select 'Recording' in the left panel. Click on the list beside 'Store my recordings at,' select 'Choose a new location,' and select the folder or location that will collect all the recordings.

Share Your Screen

To share your screen with other participants, click on the green icon depicting 'Share Screen' at the main window's bottom.

When this window pops up, you can choose the desktop or screen that you want to share with others. As soon as you click on 'Share,' a window saying 'Allow Zoom to share your screen' will pop up. Click on 'Open System Preferences' and select 'Zoom' from the list.

End the Meeting

To end the meeting or the exit, select 'End Meeting,' denoted in red in the bottom-right corner. Select 'End Meeting for All' from the pop-up window to end the meeting.

Schedule a Meeting

Now let's try scheduling the next meeting, go to the main page of your app, and click on the icon that says 'Schedule.'

- Type the name of the subject, class, or topic of discussion of the 'Topic' box meeting. Select the starting and ending date and time of the meeting. Since we are learning the features on the free version of Zoom, you can set only 40 minutes. To increase the duration, go to the official website and buy a subscription plan that offers longer meetings and additional benefits.

- Next, select the box beside 'Generate Automatically' under 'Meeting ID' (this should be your preferred option).

- Then, generate a password by checking the box beside the 'Require a meeting password.' Type a password of your choosing and share it with the other participants to give them access to the meeting. By unchecking the box, anyone can access the meeting without a password, so it's always preferable to create a password.

- Next, you can select whether you want your video to be on or off during the meeting. You also have the option to choose whether you want your participants' video to be on or off.

- For the audio, select 'Telephone and Computer Audio,' as some of your participants might use their phone and cellular data if they don't have a stable broadband connection.

- You can add this schedule reminder on a calendar of your choice. Choose among iCal, Google Calendar, or any other calendar that you use.

- Lastly, click on Advanced Options and select your preferred option among 'Enable waiting room' (lets your participants wait before starting the meeting), (lets your participants enter the meeting before you do), 'Mute participants on entry' (mutes all participants until you enter and unmute), and 'Record the meeting automatically on the local computer' (begins recording without selecting the option).

Once you select the appropriate options, click on 'Schedule' and your meeting will be noted on your calendar. When you open your calendar, you will receive the details regarding the meeting, including the meeting ID, password, and even a mobile tap feature that directly takes you to the meeting if accessed through a cell phone. Send this auto-generated message containing the meeting details to your desired participants through e-mail or text.

Schedule

Chapter 4: 5 Best Hidden Features of Zoom

The Zoom platform is an excellent answer to video interaction and communication problems faced by businesses and large organizations. The platform comprises of several essential scales and attributes. It is, therefore, important to understand several tips and tricks of the program. Below are a few tricks that you should know to improve your experience:

Use Virtual Background

The platform consists of various attributes, but this is a wonderful one. It let users attach a custom background to their project. It could be in the form of materials like an image or video in the course of the interaction. It also provides several out of box media, and users can include their video or picture to the background of their project.

The program can differentiate between the background and the face of the user in real-time. You must allow the feature if you want to utilize it. Select the Cogswell logo to launch settings and navigate to the virtual background. In this section, you can decide what type of image you want to display on your background. You can choose several available options.

Enhanced Beauty

The platform can help users prepare for the intended meeting by beautifying them. It has an attribute with the name touch my appearance. It is a filter that adds smoothness to the surface of the skin. It is not an aggressive filter and also make minimal modification to the face. You can hardly notice the difference. It keeps the natural look of the face, and you can set it up before participating in the video interaction. You can perform that task with a few clicks. Follow the below steps:

1. Launch the app.

2. Select the gear logo beneath the picture of the account.

3. Tap video.

4. Tick the touch my appearance box.

5. Mute and un-mute mic.

It is one of the most interesting attributes of the platform. It gives users the power to minimize and eradicate background noise and cross-talks, especially when there are lots of attendants on the video interaction. You can perform this task with a simple click.

For instance, if you find yourself in a conference on the web and have nothing to contribute at that moment, you can easily mute your mic. Whenever you want to contribute, you can turn it back on for usage. You can turn it on by holding your space bar, which will turn on the mic, and you can start talking. If you take your hands off the space bar, the mic goes mute again.

The feature ensures that you have a smooth interaction without interruptions and do not take lots of bandwidth. It also offers excellent clarity of voice, which means that everyone can hear each other. If you want to utilize this attribute, launch settings, select audio, and allow mute mic anytime you want to join an interaction. It makes the whole process easy and straightforward.

Disallow Video When You Want to Join a Video Interaction

At some point in time, you might get a video alert and join the call quickly without preparation. The platform offers a solution to fix that problem. The disallow feature can save you from that embarrassment. There is an option for you to disallow the feature permanently anytime you want to link up with an interaction. Whenever you are fit enough to face the camera, you can turn it back on and utilize it. If you want to utilize this attribute, navigate to your settings, and launch it, select the video and turn my video off anytime, I join a meeting.

Allow Gallery View

There are several attributes that the platform comprises, but you are going to love and admire this one. It keeps everyone on one page, and you 'keep track of all the attendants' in the interaction in one place at a time. You can also utilize this attribute anytime you put together small groups, and you must turn it on if you want to use it. To allow it, select a gallery view, and you can enjoy the outstanding experience it offers.

Automatically Copy Invitation URL

If you want to invite lots of attendants to your video interaction, you must utilize a global attribute that the platform offers, which you can utilize to copy invitation URL and place it on your clipboard. You can save lots of time by selecting invite and locating the URL for it.

So launch settings and toggle general, then allow automatically copy URL anytime the interaction begins. You can start sending the invites to attendants that you want to participate by distributing the link to social media and several platforms with ease.

Chapter 5: Zoom for Teachers

Require Self-Identification

When using Zoom, it is sometimes impossible to meet members to see the person who is hosting the meeting. It is important to see the person who is talking as the person's body language may provide more clues into understanding the subject matter. Imagine a scenario in which meeting members introduce themselves by saying their names before sharing a thought o asking a question. Until people in a meeting become familiar with the person heading a meeting, a certain level of communication may not be achieved.

Make Proper Use of the Microphone

This step is very important because it ensures that everyone participating in a Zoom meeting or lecture is carried along. Persons participating in a meeting may also have to make use of the Chat functionality to pass a request to the person chairing a meeting to get them unmuted so that they can pass information to the other participants. Most video conferencing rooms have a provision for a microphone. A microphone ensures that all sounds from one part of the conferencing room that is directly in contact with the microphone are heard in other parts of the room. These include side commenting, whispering, sneezing, eating, page-turning tapping, pencil, a sound made while eating, etc.

Set a Standard of Protocol

When setting a standard protocol for a Zoom meeting, some of these points will help you make the meeting more effective:

- Do not indulge in shuffling paper, side communication, noisemaking, and tapping pens. When this is done, the microphone can easily pick it. Then, it will be a major distraction to the other participants of the meeting. For these reasons, it is a best practice to turn off the microphone functionality so that any member who has something important to say can indicate in the chat feature so that they can be unmuted to speak.

- To avoid causing distractions to others, it is also in your best interest not to engage in activities like drinking, eating, and chewing gum.

- Strive to make eye contact with the person chairing a meeting when he/she is talking by focusing on the position where the camera is, as this will help you in positioning yourself better to learn more.

- To encourage the instructor, it may be a nice try nodding your head and paying close attention to the information that he/she is passing across.

- When you want to ask a participant a question, directly state their name to have them give you their attention. To this end, it is important to get yourself familiarized with the participants before the start of the meeting.

Participating in a Meeting On Camera

Put the following points in the back of your head when you are participating in a Zoom meeting or video conference on camera:

- Ensure that you are already set for the lecture or meeting a few minutes before the start of the meeting. If you are the meeting's chairperson, this is a particularly important step as it helps you test the video and audio connections to ascertain if they are functional.

- Mute your microphone when you are not speaking to students at remote sites. Also, have students at all sites mute their microphones when they are not speaking to avoid feedback.

- When you are not directly speaking to any participant in the meeting, it is a wise decision to have your microphone muted. This step will help you contain any disturbance on your part.

- If you are the instructor, keep eye contact with the rest of the participants at different locations. Make sure that you create unnecessary attention for someone by selecting, staring at him/her only. If possible, let your gaze be random, but let it carry the same effect as when you will talk to just one person.

Also, when speaking, speak though you are in a conventional face-to-face meeting or lecture. Close doors and windows, off your cell phones, turn off the noise that emanates from your computer to keep off unnecessary sounds.

- During the process of delivering a presentation, sharing videos, files, or images, do not forget to give the grace of 2-3 seconds or a delay in transmission. You can also do this with audios. When you are done commenting, pause to allow the other meeting members to assimilate and respond to the message before continuing to the next visual or discussion.

- Make it a routine to check the level of coherence of the meeting participants to see if they can hear and understand what you are communicating.

Collaboration and Pedagogy Ideas

When you are preparing for a Zoom meeting, let these ideas be your ideals.

- Make sure that you have a clear idea of what you want to share. You may also like to consider availing a schedule or plan for each meeting to the participants to make the meeting a smooth and comprehensive one. When this is done, it is almost always a certainty that the meeting's object will be achieved. Each plan/class agenda can reiterate the desired etiquette.

- Discuss your plan and schedule. Keep yourself within the intended series of events and have it at the back of your mind to keep the meeting participants engaged.

- Inquiry and Questioning. As explained before, reserve some time to explain some concepts or discussion of certain topics for the benefit of your class of participants. When you put this into, give the participants the benefit of time to dish out their response. It may often take time, and network connectivity may interfere with how fast you get to hear them when they eventually speak. Participants ought to provide their feedback to their instructors to both parties on the same page and help them not be lost during a sound video conference.

- Breakout Groups. Before significant group conversation, consider offering a small amount of class time for a group activity or using the "think-pair-share" technique to have participants.

- Let participants make use of annotation tools during conferencing.

- Sometimes, make the participants the presenter to allow them to share their thoughts, projects, ideas, etc. with the rest of the participants.

Concepts for Utilizing Zoom as a Screencasting Tool

- Create annotated and narrated mini-lectures and slide lectures.

- Create introductions and overviews for courses if that is the object of the meeting.

- Create tutorials and screen recordings for web tours, filling out forms, software programs, etc.

Some Tricks for Utilizing Zoom for Screencasting

- Keep video lessons/segments short.

- Use animations, images, and visuals economically when they assist in passing a message.

- Keep text on a slide or page to the lowest when projecting text. When the text becomes too much, or too small so that they don't fit into one page or slide, they will become almost impossible to read through Zoom screen sharing.

- Use the annotation tools of Zoom to point out certain information or bring student's attention to a major point.

- Create embedded or guided activities or questions for the participants to do when they are done watching a video. But then, this is entirely a function of the intent of the meeting in the first place.

Create and Flow a Gathering Plan and Notes

Gatherings with a reliable calendar advantage enormously from a setup plan and meeting notes. If somebody veers off, the gathering host or co-host can allude back to the gathering plan. It's typical for gatherings to a table or sideline discussion on an issue that goes excessively far from the expected gathering objective.

Beneficial gatherings have plans that are circulated ahead of time and, as often as possible, utilize a common report for recording meeting notes. If a fruitful discussion begins to crash the first plan, a host can make a note of the data and table the discussion for a survey at the next gathering. It's useful to share meeting notes in a sorted-out envelope on a common drive that all gathering individuals' approach. Additionally, posting the notes in a cooperation channel that all individuals from the gathering are a piece of is a great method to keep ventures pushing ahead.

Learn to Tune In

Figuring out how to be a decent audience is another vital aspect for facilitating gainful gatherings. Hosts who do the vast majority of the talking need to make sure to take a delay, inhale, and tune in. A decent gathering host will stop and request a contribution from other gathering participants. Progressing from talking mode to listening mode is additionally significant for all gathering participants. However, an investigation from Psychology Today finds that solitary 10 percent of individuals effectively tune in during most discussions (Osten, 2016). At times the most significant thing you can do is tune in.

Tuning in to and drawing in with other gathering members deferentially and nicely is significant. Close listening additionally can empower you to publicly support new thoughts since we gain from others' encounters. Compelling pioneers comprehend the significance of good tuning in, and they appreciate it. Regardless of whether you see yourself as the "educator" in your gathering, urge others to decipher and distill the data they've assimilated and shared it during a gathering.

Attempt a PechaKucha Presentation

Looking for a little motivation? Have a go at facilitating a PechaKucha introduction. PechaKucha, which signifies "chatter" in Japanese, is a method of introducing a story in only 400 seconds with 20 pictures. Each picture gets 20 seconds during the almost seven-minute introduction. The thought behind PechaKucha is to introduce basic data as fast as conceivable to keep crowds occupied with a narrating procedure that they can without much of a stretch comprehend.

The PechaKucha introduction group offers an unmistakable start, center, and end to the story. Since each slide is allowed precisely 20 seconds, the crowd knows where they are in the story. This introduction style offers setting on introduction length for conceivably restless crowds. PechaKucha forces request on narrating and gives the crowd a timetable to reference.

While PechaKucha may not be the correct decision for each gathering, it exhibits the intensity of request in an introduction setting. A plan can also force a settled upon request that will assist gatherings with remaining on target and stay beneficial. In the following part, you'll find out about gathering behavior and the significance of voice value.

Chapter 6: Tips and Tricks to Motivate Students to Take Lessons

Inspiration is, in all actuality, one of the basic mainstays of a fruitful classroom. As a mentor, you're never going to achieve your objective without moving your understudies. Inspiration is certifiably not an entangled idea, and it's anything but a troublesome activity to spur the understudies. We live our lives with satisfaction and joy, with torment and distress, since we are motivated to push ahead. Better believe it, regularly being disregarded and disappointed in our lives, we keep away from our expectation of pushing ahead. Yet, when the human instinct is empowered, we begin to reconsider pushing ahead. Similarly, as a rule, without being animated, the understudy loses would like to learn. That is the reason understudies should be propelled.

An educator can't be a decent instructor, except if he realizes how to move a student. An astounding teacher is an individual who knows the realities and strategies of how to make a functioning classroom, where the understudy can partake excitedly. As a general rule, you won't have the option to satisfy your sole duty without inspiring your understudies.

There is an assortment of ways to deal with rouse understudies in the homeroom. Probably the best thoughts for empowering the understudies in the school are talked about underneath. As a general rule, these tips on persuading your understudies can help you make your classroom progressively beneficial and innovative.

Guarantee Anxiety-Free Classroom

What do you know? Dread additionally represses learning results. Along these lines, never try to force fear by authorizing disciplines in your classroom. I have discovered that a few of us, the educators, are executing additional assignments as a discipline, because physical controls don't happen in showing today, as in the old and traditional period. Likewise, negative comments regularly offer ascent to fear among understudies in the classroom. Regardless of whether it's for revenge or compromising remarks, the dread in the classroom will never motivate the students. In all actuality, dread is a hindrance to taking an interest effectively in the learning meeting. The understudy ought to never look to take a functioning part in the classroom. That is the reason each educator ought to keep up a dread free class to rouse the understudies. Along these lines, they never offer negative expressions and troubling errands as disciplines.

Promote Their Ideas and Decisions

To advance innovative learning in the homeroom. Even though it is offering assignments and coursework, giving them their opportunity to pick the subject all alone, your understudies will be motivated. You know, all things considered, that individuals need appreciation. Truly, thankfulness changes a lot of understudies' lives. Your understudies can't hold on to partake in your next talk. What's more, if you appreciate new thoughts, several incredible thoughts will likewise be presented to different understudies in your homeroom. So consistently welcome new plans to motivate your understudies.

Explain the Objective

Each understudy enjoys clear guidelines. Explain every objective and target objective to be cultivated toward the start of the course. Remember to refer to the impediments they may look during the meeting. Examine potential cures about the difficulties they may confront. Subsequently, they will be propelled to address more issues, which will make the subject progressively available. Accordingly, you will find that your homeroom has become fruitful because your understudies are empowered.

"As an instructor, you are setting up a nation, another world that will come before long guideline you and the earth."

Improve the Environment of the

Classroom

Don't generally plunk down to talk about the exercise. Move next to the students and consider the experience. Keep them out of your group once in a while. Instruct them to visit the library now and again for investigation purposes. The move in the classroom condition animates the learning cerebrum's energy, which is essential for inspiration.

Be a Good Listener

Listen cautiously to what your understudy needs to state. Value their feelings and conclusions. Find a way to take care of the issues they talk about. Be an incredible audience, fellow. They're going to begin adoring you when you hear them out with legitimate consideration. You will win their certainty, hence. Presently, is it difficult to move them? You need to hear them out first on the off chance that you need your understudies to hear you out.

Share Their Experience

Not all understudies can share their involvement with the course of the class. Understanding books will involve some of them. However, as sure understudies examine their exercises related mastery, others might be motivated to effectively take an interest. Set up the exercise in such a compelling way that different kinds of students can connect effectively in the sharing of exercises. In this circumstance, different understudies are regularly propelled to share their encounters. You can, subsequently, guarantee that the classroom is effective.

Positive Competition

The helpful rivalry is, fundamentally, a valuable system in the school. Guarantee the contention is productive. A decent contention in bunch work propels students hugely. We are additionally arranged to complete network work, which will likewise carry significant advantages to their expert life. There is no uncertainty that good rivalry sparkles energy among the understudies in the classroom.

Know Your Student Well

You have to realize your understudies well. Likewise, you ought to know their inclinations, their aversions, their viability, and their absence of execution. At the point when your understudies understand that you realize them well, they will start to like you and reveal their hindrances. It would be simpler for you to motivate your understudies correctly. You won't have the option to energize them since you realize them well.

Support Them and Give Them Responsibility

Give them the obligation of the understudies. Allot them a class venture. They're going to work with assurance without a doubt. In such a circumstance, singular understudies may likewise need to satisfy their commitments. When you give them obligations, trust inside themselves will develop, and they will start to feel that they are significant because they get an incentive from you. They would then be propelled to connect more in the classroom. At the point when you confide in them, they will consistently confide in you consequently.

Show Your Enthusiasm

To convey your excitement in the classroom during a talk while meeting your obligations. Offer your energy about their extraordinary achievement. Once more, it shows a romantic premium when each student presents another thought. Your demeanor of excitement will empower them.

Hold Your Record

Compose a report for you. Record each achievement of your understudy. On the off chance that you locate that a particular understudy is changing, address the understudy about change. Show the understudy the record. Rewards and bolster the understudy before the classroom. Indeed, even offer the progressions with your companions, on the off chance that an understudy finds that you're dealing with the understudy. At the same time, your address from your record and the understudy is enlivened.

Valuable Feedback

On the off chance that an understudy isn't progressing nicely, incorporate positive input. At the point when important, offer another opportunity. Be a companion and look to comprehend the instance of such an awful outcome. Urge the understudy to rouse him/her to improve rapidly next time, as he/she didn't see how to do well in this subject with legitimate information and procedure. All right, guess what? Your valuable surveys will change many lives. Take a gander best case scenario understudies in your school; you will get a lot of good characteristics. Advise them regarding the delightful conditions they have. As a general rule, esteem them, which will rouse them altogether consequently.

Real-life Situation in the classroom

Relate your exercise plan to an actual situation. Make the exercise charming with the fun of the game. Reveal to it an astounding story with a blend of amusingness. The perusing along these lines makes it feasible for the understudy to react to their understanding. Let them likewise apply the exercise to their understanding. Just track it precisely. In actuality, when you're managing your perusing, in actuality, situations, understudies are urged to learn and go to your group.

Bottom Line

An educator must guarantee that the classroom is dynamic. Educators should not say that they can simply enter and leave the homeroom with 'Great Stories' without giving an effective class. Through rousing your understudies, you can make the best classroom you're anticipating. Just like an educator, you are setting up a nation, another world that will come before long principle you and the planet.

Communicate With Your Parents and Guardians

Utilize the homeroom to keep the guardians and gatekeepers on the up and up. You should welcome guardians to pursue an ordinary or week-by-week email overview of what's happening in their kids' schools. Messages contain the pending or incomplete work of an understudy, just as updates and questions that you post in the class stream.

Allotting Assignments to a Group of Students

Instructors may designate work and post-declarations to singular understudies or a gathering of understudies in a class. This usefulness encourages instructors to recognize guidance as required, just as to advance community-oriented gathering work.

Utilizing the Classroom Mobile App Annotations

Understudies and instructors can utilize the Mobile Classroom on Android, iOS, and Chrome cell phones. You can give a contribution to constant by explaining the understudy's work in the application. Understudies may likewise record their assignments to pass on a thought or idea without any problem.

Explore the Integration of Classroom With Other Resources

Google Classroom utilizes an API to connect and trade information with an assortment of your preferred gadgets. Many utilizations and sites are fused, similar to Pear Deck, Actively Read, Newsela, and many, some more.

Chapter 7: Build Real Connection to Your Students

Eligible online educators often worry that virtual teaching is more about making a good learning experience and not just about the mechanics of distance learning—no matter what the setting of learning is. Despite that, getting to know their students is very challenging for some online teachers. It happens when an online class has 20 and above students at a time. So, if the course is online, with no eye-to-eye connections, then how can you build individual connections? There are various proven ways to work around the issue. I pulled up some of them to help you navigate building connections with your students.

As an online instructor, building a strong connection with your students is crucial because there is no visual aid to help you see all of them at once during a class. While a couple of the students in the class are noisy, the rest of them may stay quiet. This means it is easy for you to overlook the students who are not actively communicating.

Thus, it turns out to be extremely difficult for you to know which student is doing some other thing, sleeping, incapable of seeing the course layout, or just generally lost. It happens in an online course that neglects to include an important learning key, i.e., personal connection with the instructor.

Without an important connection with you, your students can get confused and may feel detached. It makes them less motivated, and they begin to lose interest in the course.

Principles

Online classes can be a lot like conventional study halls in which a couple of students do a large portion of the talking, and others never make a single sound. When a course is 100% online with no eye-to-eye contact, what principles would you be able to apply to cause individual connections to occur?

Try Out One-on-One Communication Options

Setting up these connections on an individual level requires some effort. Here are some credible methods you can try:

- **Introductions**: Most online courses include a type of early introduction, for example, a conversation discussion that expects students to post something important to them, as a way of getting to know one another better.

- **Discussion Boards**: This may not be possible to react to each student's post each week. This methodology isn't really attractive either. They may give you another way of concentrating on different individual students every week.

- **Email**: All over your course, there are various points when you or your students have to start an email discussion. It can be a good way to check on a student when you notice there have not been active or he/she is missing assignments.

- **Make it meaningful**: A personal connection with your students is a higher priority than creative conversations. Everyone is occupied with work, school, and family responsibilities, so adding prerequisites for connection for the sake of just adding them is counterproductive.

- **Consider class size and time**: Be realistic about what you can achieve, given the number of students in your course and the amount of time you need to work with them. Large registrations, as well as shorter learning times, make individual connections nearly impossible. Alter your expectations appropriately and consider what you can do with little groups to cultivate a connection and communication.

- **Plan ahead**: Make plans to learn and adapt for both you and your students and continue working on clear communication systems.

- **Practice**: Challenge yourself to make these individual connections, yet allow time for slow adaptation. Start gradually with new methods to know what works for you and your students, and don't be hesitant to get some information about their interests and expectations as well. The same way you adjust your content and materials before every lesson, you can also try new ways to deal with communication.

Small Teaching Online Quick Tip: Building Connections

Here are a few tips for building connections with your students:

Introduce Yourself

Create a feeling of cooperation and connection between your students and yourself by starting the first conversation. Try to make this meeting by inspiring conversation as far as learning and individual goals of students, their strengths, and other additional characteristics.

You can begin by posting a short bio of yourself. It may include your area of specialization, background, interests, and your most recent photograph. It will make your students feel that you are a good teacher, and they will follow your example and use it as an aid to guide them in sharing information about themselves with the rest of the class.

It is one of the best ways to connect with the students in your online classroom and to know their interests. You can also use Google Forms to gather information on your students, find out about their interests, background, educational abilities, and learning preferences. Another smart idea is to dedicate a particular part of your course site for posting pictures and brief profiles of all of your students.

Or then again, even better, you can ask your students to create a quick personal mindset board that they can share with you and the rest of the class. For this, you ask them to use a few accessible online mindset-mapping instruments.

Adapt Your Course

One of the best ways to amplify the individual connection and to expand the capability of eLearning is to adapt your course. When we say adapt the course, we mean structure it in a way that incorporates human connection.

An adapted course is bound to establish a relationship between you and your students, and this can be accomplished in several ways.

Influence Online Conversations

Give the students a conversation platform. Providing an online conversation board contributes to relating with friends and fellow students and in getting important feedback. Because of this, the best choice is to go with an online platform that you are familiar with—one that is easily reachable to your students. Additionally, you can use the conversation boards' tool, or perhaps you can create a Facebook group and ask your students to join.

Advance Multimedia With Personalization

Media fused courses empower the various kinds of students to meet their personal needs. Various students have diverse learning styles, so the ideal approach to furnishing them with useful learning resources is through sight and sound. You may utilize YouTube and assist visual students with videos. Also, give a digital podcast to students who learn better with sound and intuitive games for students who do better through gamification of learning.

But, if you wish to get intuitive and precise feedback, you should make video updates and video presentations on your course. These videos may include:

- Discussions regarding next week's assignments and their specific subtleties. Additionally, best practices and questions from students regarding different assignments.

- Discussions about the lessons of the past week or any information that needs any update or support.

- More information to the primary content: some industry-based tips and hacks.

- You could make on-the-spot learning through VoiceThread, for your students to be able to collaborate with you and each other during interpretation.

All of this will help keep your audiovisual course fascinating, and it will also help improve your students' understanding.

Foster Collaborative Learning

This teaching strategy is a brilliant method to increase the motivation of students to learn. It happens through group learning. In this teaching strategy, a small group of students collaborates on a specific project or task.

Henceforth, the responsibility for and teaching is shared by the group of students. It gives your students substantially more chances to actively take part in their learning, ask questions, and evaluate one another. Furthermore, your students will show signs of improvement and willingness to share; they will talk about their thoughts directly and apply what they have learned and are learning.

If you design the exercises carefully, you can help your students learn the skills they need to work as a team effectively. These organized conversations additionally help to avoid arguments and fights.

Another way to avoid these contentions is to encourage your students to speak with one another and to have important conversations. Also, create a classroom that would promote a safe platform for meaningful and attentive conversations—including questions to offer ascent to result-oriented arguments.

Engage Them in Decision Making

Nothing could be more empowering than permitting an individual to become a part of important decision-making processes. While this is a typical practice in the business world to enable workers to feel drawn in, the same practice can also be used in building stronger connections with your online students. So, let your students partake in the decision-making process of the class. For example, allow them to pick the projects they are going to do or the specific points you will examine in a personal essay. The most important thing is that you make them feel they are a real part of the online teaching course. To do this, you can make use of Survey Monkey to find out about students' supposition, or you may simply add a few evaluations to your eLearning course.

Support Intelligent Communication

The most direct way to promote connection is to support intelligent communication. It may include texting or live chats.

Encourage your students to benefit as much as possible from whatever form of intelligent conversations you all decide on, whether it is moderated conversations or off and on conversations. Encourage them to leverage on this opportunity to connect you as well as with their schoolmates, concerning their project conversations or group projects.

Define Your Student Reward System

Prizes are a great way to keep your students motivated. It causes them to be more interested in the course, helping them to focus on learning. Since individuals acknowledge rewards, a lot of teachers benefit as much as possible from remunerations systems to get the attention of their students. These prizes can be given at the end of projects or group exercises.

Another approach to connect with your students is to consider their suggestions when choosing the prize. An award for finishing the course of action will persuade your students to invest greater energy in learning, and they will consistently stay connected with you and focused on the course's goals.

As an online instructor, all your students need to have the ideal learning involvement with your courses. A personal connection between you and a student can influence their levels of commitment, as well as information retention and success. Creating personalized communication opportunities and building a connection, while both basic parts of online teaching, are not the same. Personalized communication is only one way to build positive connections with your online students.

Chapter 8: Common Zoom Problems and How to Fix Them

Five Common Zoom Problems and How to Fix Them

Zoom isn't left out when it comes to having problems of its own which can be solved in a few steps. Some of these problems are:

1. Webcam or Audio Not Working

Sometimes, you join a meeting only to discover that there's no video or audio feed from your end. The first step toward avoiding this is to make sure to always enter a meeting by clicking on the Join with Video option. Other times, Zoom simply doesn't have access to your video or audio input because they are in use in another program or application. It's advised to close down such applications first before joining a meeting on Zoom. In other instances, the lack of video or audio feed from your device can be because you haven't granted Zoom permission to use your device camera and microphone yet. The solution is to ensure that Zoom has permission to do so in the in-app permission settings.

2. Echoes During a Call

Another common problem with Zoom is audio echo during a meeting. There could be three reasons for echoes during a meeting. One, an attendee may leave both computer and telephone audio on at the same time. To solve this, ask them to switch either the telephone audio or computer audio off. Another cause of echoes during meetings is having computer or telephone speakers too close to each other. It is either you switch one source of audio off, or you keep both very far apart. Finally, having many computers with active audio in the same room could cause echoes especially if they are close together. Ask the computer users to stay apart or use a headphone to solve this.

3. Problems Sharing a Screen

Sharing your screen is an important part of a Zoom call and is as easy as clicking Share Screen at the bottom of the window. Before you try to share your screen during a meeting, ensure that you are connected to the meeting and you have a strong internet connect. Sharing screens is a bandwidth consuming activity.

You can also solve this by starting the meeting on audio only while sharing your screen. This is done by selecting Start with No Video at the Home tab when joining or starting a meeting. If have already begun a video meeting, and you have trouble sharing your screen, switch off your video. This saves bandwidth. Use the Stop Video button and then click on the Share Screen to share your screen.

4. Problems Receiving Email Messages From Zoom

Another common problem many users face is that they do not receive email messages from Zoom. This includes notifications and activation mails. These usually take 30 minutes to arrive and could take longer, but if it doesn't arrive, you need to make sure that your email is configured properly. Usually, this isn't something on your end, so you'll need to ask your IT department to whitelist Zoom's email IP addresses. If you're using Gmail or a personal emailing service, you can check your spam account, too.

5. Missing Features

If popular features including the ability to share a portion of your screen with attendees don't appear in your account, there's nothing to worry about. You've likely joined a meeting with a browser instead of the dedicated app. Although Zoom works in browsers, the functionality of the web version is limited compared to what you get when you use the application. The time required to connect to a meeting is also much longer, and in some cases, the connection is not established at all. To resolve this issue and access all of the features offered by Zoom, download the Zoom app to your device and always use it to host or join a meeting.

Chapter 9: Advantages and Disadvantages

Zoom is one of the most quickly increasing video conferencing technologies out there. Installation and hosting of video calls are fast. It is perfect for video chats with friends and family or conferencing with your staff when operating from home. There are many benefits of using Zoom in your teaching and remote working in this scenario.

Benefits of Zoom

Unless the business is like the other, all of its workers are operating right now from home because of the current scenario all over the world. It will usually find teamwork incredibly challenging. Software solutions such as Zoom, however, communicate nature and extent. You might use Zoom to hold a community meeting with all of your staff regardless of where each participant is. Additionally, you can hold one-on-one meetings, workshops for employee training, and more through the Zoom website. Such critical technologies make it easier for management practitioners to link and involve their diverse teams and keep their businesses going productively forward.

Zoom has several useful functionality tools. Yet fortunately, because of the elegant Zoom design, these functions are simple to use. Many of the features of the video conferencing system are readily available. They need limited instruction to allow full use of them. When you want to get lost, the Zoom page provides loads of support tools. Finally, Zoom is helpful because it does not charge you to use your corporation. It is pretty cheap, in fact, regarding the abundance of characteristics it comes with. You can use functions for free though Zoom still provides premium plans with comprehensive feature sets. But, even these are not going to make any difference, ensuring good return on investment for the organizations that use it.

Remote Working

We are trying to maintain things stable while the condition is not usually challenging—particularly during global crises. One such thing is to change roles and work from home while we are used to going to the workplace every day. In these days of video calling, tweeting, and file sharing, several people are happily willing to transfer their workdays early. Nonetheless, remote work has been a part of the daily lifestyle of many cultures for years. Although the transition may seem challenging, it is not impossible. Developers take on our staff's technology strategies and the knowledge of many of our reporters and editors to put together information and suggestions from home on having worked. It involves both detailed information about working remotely, having to deal with conference calls, and make a decent standing desk, but also quick tips on how to utilize Zoom. Zoom can help in organizing class meetings and staff meetings sitting at home. It can help you to work remotely no matter where you are and what you are doing.

Work From Home

Remote job and teaching more effective are becoming increasingly common in schools and businesses around the globe, and institutions need to ensure their employees have the techniques they need to get the best communications experience at home. Zoom is introducing the unveiling of the latest category, Zoom, for Home, as part of our commitment to helping anyone operating from home, which enables you to access a dedicated personal communication tool for video presentations, phone calls, and immersive whiteboard. Each group incorporates updates to the Zoom app with compatible equipment for improving the home business experience.

Zoom for Home is also compliant with all Zoom Rooms Devices, like Sleek and Poly hardware options, enabling consumers to pick the equipment they need to build the ideal work-from, home connectivity experience through spaces including the family room. Sign in to a computer compliant with Zoom for Home with a Zoom user profile to immediately create interactive office environments with no additional licenses (Zoom for Home is eligible for all Zoom discussion licenses, except Basic).

- Easily schedule meetings, work collaboratively virtually with information sharing, annotation, and send and receive telephone calls.

- Synchronizes with the user's schedule, status, conference settings, and phone for an embedded video-first identity management experience.

- Zoom for home computers may be established for virtual IT control through the admin app.

- Ensures the equipment is primarily developed for simple operation with minimal or no IT assistance is suited for desk configurations and matches the price level for setting up a home workplace.

A Chance to Work on Your Passion

If you should do one thing to change your life, it is doing what you are excited about and using it as a profession, as a career, or as a passion. While this is not easy, the path is worth it because it pays off when you are doing something that you enjoy. It is not easy to work on your passion while attending a hectic routine. A tiring job or a student routine can make you keep your passion aside. During the current scenario, there is a lot of time for everyone to take a stand and work hard on passion while staying at home using Zoom. It can help you to learn different things and taking classes in different short courses. Zoom provides excellent benefits for its users, especially in the learning process.

Good for Online Teaching

As a teacher, if you or your learners have a situation that keeps you from meeting the person, Zoom can help maintain your class going. Online class meetings, in which everyone is planned to join a Zoom meeting, are one way to create interaction when learners are remote. Still, Zoom can also be used to assist other learning and teaching situations. So long as a student attendant is on a laptop, they can select a connection to the URL and be taken to a chat with the instructor instantly. It removes slow updates entirely, annoying bonus services, and plenty of boring things. Often people need to upgrade their software or flash to reach, but that never transforms into an issue that lasts more than two minutes. It is suitable for first-time gatherings and already-off meetings. Zoom provides different beneficial features for online classes like a whiteboard, screen sharing, screen recording, assignment and presentation setup, etc.

Chapter 10: Is Online Learning as Effective as Face-To-Face Learning?

In the recent past, the only study option was a face-to-face study. But now, with technology growing, online education is becoming increasingly common. But, you may also have some reservations regarding its efficacy. While online degrees empower you to learn at a rate that fits in and around you and the responsibilities, they're also a perfect way to quickly develop your employable skills without losing your paycheck to your studies.

For years, face-to-face instruction has become the norm, and it is reasonable to believe that online education cannot compete with that. Two general beliefs are that people cannot remember knowledge acquired digitally or take education positively when performed online. So, it's important to look at some points which indicate the effectiveness of online education.

Today, several businesses, colleges, wealthy businessmen, staff, and students understand the value of e-learning. Compared with conventional classes, online classes are a flexible, easier, and immersive way to know.

But, before you get aboard the e-learning bus, take some time to understand how online learning measures up against conventional face-to-face approaches to see if it sits perfectly for you. The sheer number of learners enrolling in online degree programs has grown significantly in recent years—and with online education becoming more relevant than ever as the environment responds to the problems presented by the Covid-19 outbreak, we will discuss how online schooling stacks up against face-to-face study.

So yes, studying online is pretty common, and it' sits not hard to see why. Yet is it truly more efficient and effective than the conventional method? Let's have a peek at the reasons why digital learning is better than learning face to face, or at least as good as traditional education.

1. Engagement With the Content

Concentrating around for a complete two-hour lesson is difficult. However, online classes may be broken down into smaller pieces along the process, with skills tests. The method called microlearning ensures an individual can initiate and conclude a topic within a period of five to ten minutes. It is not only useful, but evidence frequently shows that microlearning improves note-taking and reduces interruption.

2. High Levels of Retention

For digital approaches, the volume of knowledge acquired equals that of conventional face-to-face approaches. E-learning lets users train at their own pace and in their manner. Considering these elements of online education, along with enhanced participation, support the consolidation of information.

As per the Research Institute of America, e-learning may improve information retention by 25-60 percent. It is because electronic instructional resources stimulate visually, are succinct, and are more engaging. Additionally, elements such as game-based learning, polls, questionnaires, and tests found in a typical LMS render it much more social. Online classes increase the success rate of the staff as opposed to conventional classes. When courses are more immersive with interactive material (images, photos, audios, connections, etc.) and are readily available on any computer, they even allow you greater power over how you carry information into yourself. Therefore, the workers are willing to work through their speed, quicker than a conventional path.

3. Inherent Flexibility

It is significant as hectic schedules and minimal spare time are some of the factors for many not enrolling in conventional courses. However, the learners have complete control of their education through online classes. They may read and reread the course materials and use electronic tools accessible, such as electronic books, audiobooks, interactive videos, blog posts, etc. This versatility helps the students to study at their own pace and skill.

Virtual training services are more versatile in design, usually serving people who work either part-time or full-time. Students may watch on-the-go video lecturers while driving, particularly if they are mobile-friendly.

Rather than in-class assignments that may be overwhelming to others because they take more time to absorb new content, online classes allow you to complete tasks at your speed.

Students should adapt them to their current obligations and commitments, and they may interact with digital content and instructional resources at whatever time they increasingly deem most convenient. Much better: they don't have to go somewhere to learn. They can sign in from the absolute convenience of their own four walls or workplace to the virtual school.

4. Collaboration and Social Learning

For conventional approaches that only require face-to-face or phone communication, interactive and collaborative education is not feasible. Virtual learning calls for involvement in public groups online. You will do sessions in the interactive school; add electronic books and other files. Throughout the world of online networking, this sort of digital forum would allow the employees to enjoy, retweet, and vote on the course material. We should post their thoughts, questions, and doubts. Therefore, starting a thread of conversation with teachers and other learners will help create enjoyable experiences and expand the learning outside the course's structured setting.

5. Enhanced Learning

For online courses utilizing digital materials, the students gain five times more information than in conventional face-to-face classes. Since online classes provide students with complete autonomy of their learning, students may operate at their speed. Students usually operate harder than they would otherwise, and take in more details. They will move quickly around areas of course in which they are good but slower for others that they require some more time.

6. Affordable

The typical college life can be costly, no matter whether you have to stay on campus or lease a neighboring apartment. You may also pay travel costs because you have moved out of your existing hometown to join a college. So, several students consider that by taking online courses and staying at home, they can save time. They will have to pay rent, of course, so that they will save on relocation costs, college-related expenditures, special equipment costs, commuting fees, and other large price tag items.

Chapter 11: Effective Use of Zoom App

Some in-office departments will not be able to deal with video conferencing and the potential difficulties that it presents. Here are some tips to help group members conduct Zoom conferences and call seamlessly to make you more comfortable. Set aside some room for your first lesson to expose the students to the Zoom and make sure their audio and video connections.

- Have an objective or schedule by Screen Sharing a paper or slide at the beginning of the course for each lesson. It adds up to students have a clear idea of how the class will proceed, what is going to be covered, and the tasks they are going to engage in.

- Explore web behavior and student standards in the first simulated lesson, then refresh the topics daily.

- Use a shared document in the whiteboard or transcribe it, and let your learners also engage.

- Where to share a whiteboard, paper, screen, or photograph, seek math problems with whiteboarding, or let participants use annotation.

- Identify items like grammar errors in a paper you share.

- Taking the opportunity to progress the class questions, feedback, and responses. Give your users a minute to let them using answers, write in conversation, or be unmuted to ask any questions live.

- Divide the conversation into smaller units on a given topic. You may use the Breakout Room feature in Zoom on pre-assign students to attend classes for a limited period so that they can.

- Being the presenter, share the initiatives with the class. It helps the students to demonstrate what you are presenting.

- Focus on student's delivery skills as they work. It also encourages learners to hear from each other.

- Pre-arrange the meeting and silence the microphones of the member upon entry. It helps to prevent background noise and allows for your students will focus on the class.

- Aim at the monitor and get the students into eye touch. It tends to establish a more intimate link throughout teaching.

- Take a second to test your students' conversation or video to check-in and receive input from the teachers.

- Talk as though you are connected explicitly to the class while making sure you are at the proper distance to the microphone for excellent hearing performance.

- Sharing photos, files, or videos while giving a presentation offer the students a chance to loosen up or breathe in what you have shared.

- Take a break after you stop debate and encourage the students to participate before moving further.

1. Pre-Set Your Meeting

Whether you and the colleagues get over a conference depends on the planning you brought into the session. It is not a conference unless you plan. You have to be prepared for your meeting to avoid wasting time; thus, pre-plan your meeting. Before the conference starts, here are five items to do:

- Give Invites in Advance—Meetings should not be a matter of the last minute. The invitations should go at least one day in advance of a structured conference.

- Distribute the program—The program-less conference is simply a free-for-all. Create a plan and send it to the members so that they can address the subjects.

- Provide Meeting Materials—When there are advance documents that need to be checked, ensure that they are presented as early as possible so that attendants can correctly interpret them.

- Schedule Zoom Room—Make sure you arrange an appropriate meeting space that meets the number of participants and the meeting needed.

- Set Meeting Goals—Maybe the most crucial thing you should do before the meeting scheduled is the objectives of, "What is the conference's mission?" The participants want to learn why they are participating in the meeting. It lays forth a reason for the conference. Be concise about the subject of the discussion.

2. Send Invitation to Clients Directly in Calendar Using Zoom Link

Using Calendar to send direct invitations is an easy way to invite your meeting participants without sending any separate Email or text message. You can send direct invitations through the following procedure:

- Log in to the online server for the Zoom.

- Tap "Meetings" in the main pane.

- Click on "Meeting Subject."

- There are ways to add to the calendars alongside "Time."

- Clicking on "Yahoo Calendar" or "Google Calendar" would immediately create a calendar event at a particular time if you choose it.

- Clicking on Outlook Calendar will create a ."ics file" that will be loading into your calendar view.

- You can also copy the details to the conference manually by pressing the "Copy Invitation."

- When you choose "Copy Invitation," the text of the invitation to attend will open in another tab.

- Tap "Invitation to Meet" to save.

- You can copy and submit the invitation via message or elsewhere.

3. Mute Microphone when not Speaking

Ensure your microphone is muted when you are not talking. It minimizes any ambient noise or audio involvement. Use the Microphone button at the lower left of the Zoom menu that appears on the conference panel to silence the microphone. Additionally, you can configure your expectations for Zoom Meeting to automatically silence your microphone at the start of each meeting. Using the microphone button to unmute you, hold the enter key for as long as you are spoken.

This simple rule provides for seamless operation of community meetings or discussions. Use noise cancellation software to improve the audio quality to the next stage for more appropriate ambient sound reduction. Muting your microphone can help in listening to lecture attentively and control sounds that can divert your attention.

4. Inform Participants When You Record Meeting

Until capturing some audio or video conferencing, ensure all members in the meeting:

- That they are being watched.

- Are you authorized to record them?

- You may also make this request in writing, or report it at the beginning of the conference.

It not only preserves social respect but also individual businesses and regions. Consensus rules and regulations could be needed.

5. Ensure Meeting Settings Before You Start a Meeting

It is highly reasonable for video conferences to be postponed or disrupted. Turn on your computer to ensure it does not happen and test whether Zoom is functioning correctly at least ten to fifteen minutes before each meeting. Then, if anything goes wrong, alert your meeting organizer as early as possible (if you are the leader, tell your members). Although running a test before each meeting can seem stressful, it is much better than being humiliated or irritated when something terrible happens during your Zoom meeting.

6. Share Screen When Presenting

Sharing your screen helps meeting participants to understand your topic of presentation. When you are presenting or giving a lecture to your students, make sure you are sharing your screen with them. As an instructor, it will be beneficial for your learners to get an idea of the topic, and they will be able to take part in the discussion. It is not fascinating to attend lectures with voice only. Screen sharing will make speech more interesting, and you can watch any helpful video from YouTube or another website to support your topic.

7. Create a Meeting Agenda Before You Schedule a Meeting

Team members are having difficulty participating if they do not know whether they should pay attention, give their feedback, or be part of the discussion process. Still, you want their feedback; the end of the discussion is likely to infuriate everyone. Updates are best allocated and perused before the conference, using a small pane of the conference to address the participants' queries. If the aim is to make a judgment, state the rule governing the decision. Creating a meeting agenda will help you to pre-plan your meeting so that there will be more opportunities to learn instead of thinking about what to do next.

Chapter 12: The Essential Quality of an Online Teacher

The role of the teacher is to share their information through instruction and clarification. In the ordinary sense, teaching involves formal lessons on a theme, usually together with a close lesson and assessment strategies.

Teacher as Leader

Leadership comprises those items that require the teacher's interaction or involvement in ways other than content area instruction. It may include but is not limited to educating others about online learning, modeling best practices for colleagues, active participation in professional networks, and active engagement in policy initiatives.

Designer of Learning Experiences

Whether you design the entire curriculum for a course you teach, or you teach using a prepackaged curriculum, you are the deliverer of the content. You alone determine how your learners will engage with you, with each other, and with the content. It is up to you to know and understand the pedagogical approaches and strategies that are most effective for any given online lesson, including which tools are most appropriate for the delivery of that content.

A supporter of the Learning Community

The emphasis on community building in the standards is not an accident. It has become evident that engaging and supportive online learning communities create more engaged learners and produce better outcomes. And yes, collaboration is an essential element in building significant learning communities and can be facilitated in online environments.

Facilitator

Facilitators are the process flow designers. They manage the flow of discussion boards, the feedback loop, allow for the free and organized flow of information, and redirect it when learning is off-task. In effect, they orchestrate every process in the learning experience. Good facilitation takes practice, but can more easily be learned through modeling. It is always a good idea to take an online course (from an effective facilitator) before you teach an online course.

Data Analyst

Data in online environments are plentiful and can be entirely meaningful. Of course, data can consist of formative and summative assessments. Still, in an LMS, data can also consist of user tracking through visualized interfaces and dashboards. Data should be used to guide instruction and to inform parents and other stakeholders about what is working and what is not working. The good news about online teaching is that everything is transparent in an LMS. It is the perfect platform for data-driven collaboration and decision-making processes.

Educator

Facilitating an online course is both similar to and different from traditional classroom instruction. Helping learners understand the subject matter, engaging them in critical thinking through questioning, and providing support to them when needed, are necessary skills for all teachers. How these tasks are accomplished in the online classroom; however, they can be vastly different from in a traditional classroom. Online, most communication is conducted through text-based communication tools such as e-mail, chat rooms, and threaded discussion forums. Instructors need a certain level of creativity to create an environment that is safe, inviting, motivating, and engaging when they are not physically present. Commonplace verbal forms of communication are absent.

Project Manager

If you approach teaching from a traditional, teacher-centered, behaviorist viewpoint—as most of us have in the past—you should be prepared to change. Standards and guidelines on effective online teaching advocates are creating student-centered learning environments, which provide opportunities for learners to engage with the content, with you and their peers. Research supports the use of collaborative inquiry, community building, and interaction as vehicles for promoting learner motivation and engagement in online classes. Online learning is not just a different mechanism for delivering instruction. Rather, it is an opportunity to transform how teaching and learning occur.

Instructional Designer

The amount of time devoted to instructional design will depend on many factors (e.g., grade level, content area, school or program policies, etc.). Regardless, the ability to design instruction is a valuable and necessary skill, whether you teach in a face-to-face or online environment. Being an effective instructional designer requires not only knowledge and skill in the development and design of the classroom and curriculum, but also requires the ability to recognize when and how specific strategies and content are appropriate and effective.

Preparations for the online classroom include setting objectives, gathering materials, writing explanations, creating assessments, and designing multimedia presentations to illustrate complex concepts. Even when using a prepackaged curriculum, the instructor prepares in advance by becoming familiar with the content, activities, and expected student outcomes. The expected amount of activity between the instructor and the learners, as well as peer-to-peer interactions, will also influence the course design.

E-Learning Expert

Troubleshooting falls within the realm of this competency and therefore is a key skill for online instructors. Of course, you cannot know every issue that your students might encounter, but you can prepare for some common difficulties. For example, when learners experience problems logging into your classroom, having a list of fixes will come in handy.

Compassionate

Compassion begins in the soil of patience and connection, but it grows beyond that as well. I think it assumes the best. What I mean is that when a student emails to ask an annoying question, we assume that they are writing because they care about their learning. Whether we are right in our assumption or not, we will have responded with kindness and be the better for it. Something is disarming about compassion. The negligent student is often more responsive to kindness than to rigidness. Moreover, compassion does not preclude being firm. We can follow our kindness with clear and firm requirements.

Good Listener

The excellent online teacher is remembered because of their willingness to listen. But, how do you listen online? Have you ever made a hasty reply to an email, only to find out later that you had read the email too fast and missed something important? It is easy to do. Online listening often means setting aside emails until you have time to give them your full attention.

Flexible

It is a difficult one because there are always those students to whom they will take a mile if you give an inch. We fear that if we push out an assignment date, our students will stop taking due dates seriously. A massive wave of late assignments will then crash onto our desk during the final weeks of the course. The good news is that your course design and syllabus provide you with a lot of structure to lean on, making you flexible. Sometimes you may need your students to be flexible with you. That was the case for me this semester.

In your online course, that also means creating avenues of communication with your students, where they have opportunities to discuss, ask questions, and share their lives with you. That connection is your fuel to excellence as an online instructor. One of this book aims to give you starting points and strategies for developing this kind of connection with your learners.

To sum that up: it is all about teaching habits. Those habits are built on the structures you put in place, and your habits are fueled by the connection you develop with your learners.

The world of online education may be one of the most rapidly changing fields of our day. Because of that, this book will focus on more enduring topics, like habits, structures, and connections.

In considering online teaching, you may feel as if you are heading into unchartered waters. It might be helpful to compare teaching online to teaching in a brick-and-mortar setting.

While the strategies you use may be similar, you should expect to experience some differences in the amount of control you have over your classroom. As an online instructor, you must be willing to release some control, to encourage a learning community that empowers the learner. It is the most difficult transition that some instructors make, and some make it more quickly than others. With this loss of control, there comes the recognition that the strategies you are most comfortable and successful within the face-to-face classroom do not work in the online classroom. You will find it necessary to learn new ways of teaching.

Conclusion

Zoom is a great platform for meetings on the market today. It provides a regular experience for users and consists of wonderful tools that functions with each other optimally. It is a straightforward and reliable software for video conferencing and different other businesses.

Pros

Humanize interactions

It can humanize communications between attendants or conversations between employees. You must understand that a video is a collection of moving images that can be worth over one million words. The process of showing your face on the screen and looking at other attendants allows the introduction of body language charms, which is an advantage for business owners. Looking at a person while holding a conversation with them gives a good feeling and changes the nature of the interaction, it does not matter if it is a personal relationship or a business one.

Items display

It is an advantage for business and organization who loves to convince their customers. When they see the product live, it boosts their confidence and creates trust as well as convince the customer. With the utilization of the video attribute for conferencing, you can perform the task of writing on a board and displaying it so that everyone can see it.

Display the most recent and latest items that you want to sell or make an introduction of recruits that will help your business grow. The platform gives users the chance to display items that they cannot put in a suitcase or convey from one location to another for meetings on the video platform.

Internet education

There are different types of excellent courses that you will find on the internet and teachers that are ready to teach, but distance can become a problem. If you are a trainer or tutor that stays at a long distance from your students, utilizing Zoom makes the process straightforward. It is an excellent concept of obtaining and distributing knowledge without facing any problems.

Although you may not be present physically, that will not affect the task because it offers excellent communication quality. You can utilize multimedia tools, such as collaborative whiteboards and other collective tools. Another significant benefit of Zoom is that no matter the number of video call attendants, it does not diminish in quality, chats, and produces impressive sounds.

Password Problems

Many people forget their password and ID regularly, but the platform offers a solution. You do not need the requirement of a login ID or pass key to utilize the platform or worry about forgetting your details because, with few clicks, you are up running with it. It also eradicates the idea of voice blabbing and ensures that the person on the other side can hear whatever you say to them and vice versa. It is a straightforward and convenient platform to use.

Excellent audio and video service

Checking the audio or video sounds and display quality is a great way to know which platform provides the best services, and the Zoom platform is top of that category. The services that the platform offers stand out among its peers and provide excellent video services. Its quality does not diminish even in troubled locations that have low bandwidth or echo problems within its portals. It offers excellent performance and does not encounter any type of problems while in use even when the meeting attendants start joining the rooms.

Online meetings

Another great quality of the platform is the unquestionable quality of its audio and video services for several activities. The platform gives users the power to develop a URL and ID for the meeting and share it with every attendant. However, users must watch out for the usage of the central processing unit resources of the computer.

For example, during a video meeting, the processing unit can reach one hundred percent, which can be a downside because it will slow down the system and affect its performance. If you utilize the last versions of computers or at least two years old, you may not face any problems with your processing unit because it can manage HD graphics with ease and perform your task error-free.

Scalability

You must understand that the Zoom platform is expandable. It is a progressive solution, and unlike other platforms, it expands with an organization to manage the growing requirements. The ability to expand gives companies and business owners the ability to modify their interaction skills amount their employees depending on their requirements and size.

Versatility

The platform ensures that users enjoy a wonderful experience across every gadget because of its easy adaptability. It gives companies and business organizations the ability to manage every form of interaction. It does not matter if it is on a smartphone, desktops. It helps workers, managers, and customers create collaboration at any time and place using the platform, whether in a car, office, or home.

Pricing

The Zoom platform is affordable and has a great price structure for your business level and type. The pricing is a great tool for businesses and companies that want to advance their cooperation approach with little investment financially. It comes with four different plans with prices based on the number of hosts and the attributes it contains.

The plans include basic, business, professional, and enterprise. You will get a good value for your investment plan on the basics, and it is also a perfect choice for training online, sharing of the screen, inter-office meetings, and recording videos. The free version offers only forty minutes for every meeting, and it keeps each session short.

Reduces education cost

The video attribute for educational purposes saves a lot of cost for basic equipment for the process. Lots of institutions and schools in remote areas do not have the required funds to develop or enlarge educational buildings for various reasons. Utilizing the feature is an excellent option for education in such areas. It also gives the students another view of the world as well as build a new world for your pupils to see and learn things that they cannot learn in a regular class.

Improves tutor to parent's connection

Many tutors have hopes of keeping close contact with parents, which the platform made easy with the video attribute that both parties can utilize to reach one another. The concept of video meetings helps reduce misunderstandings between parents and teachers. Now tutors do not need to invite the parent to school meetings any longer. They can now utilize the platform to perform that task. Parents can always join the tutor's video meeting from any location in the world with an internet connection.

Excellent service provision on slow networks

The platform offers wonderful services across gadgets with slow networks. It can handle at least one hundred attendants at the same time. It provides a good environment for webinars and business conferences. The days of bandwidth problems are over because your data has a cloud server back up. You must know that a maximum of one hundred attendants can share the screen and execute a meaningful interaction from a remote area.

It provides a unified platform

Attendants can interact with one another whenever they want with the utilization of live chats during an interaction. It does not have a restriction on virtual or online meetings and webinars. So, anytime you want to distribute or share data or ask questions, you can perform that task with the live chat feature.

Cons

The expansion of services to the education and the business healthcare sector ensured that the Zoom platform reached its potential peak. Although the platform is the best for your business requirements, it also has its limitations, which can be a disadvantage to its users.

Many researchers have found several disadvantages of the platform, which includes infringement of privacy policy and the likes. Below are a few cons of utilizing the Zoom platform:

Expensive

Utilizing the Zoom platform incurs additional costs because there the platform comes with add-ons. You can remove that option on the basic plan level, which will make it less expensive. When you begin the addition of the extras, the price continues to go up with every inclusion.

Different plan patterns

The different platform types of plans are a benefit, but when it becomes too much, and you hardly know which one to pick. You might even think of customizing your plan. The platform comes with different types of issues for different plans. In turn, it can send customers who just want a basic plan to enjoy their services away.

Slow customer services

A representative can take about two to three days to give replies about solutions to a problem and how to fix them whenever you contact them. It can be very frustrating and can put your business at risk.

It is really hard to find an organization, business, or sector without the utilization of the Zoom platform to conduct their online meetings and video interactions among employees so you can understand why they have service delay problems.

Intrusion

The Zoom platform has a high vulnerability to cyber-attacks and hackers. Black hats can forcefully get passwords and take control over virtual and online meetings as well as post demeaning or offensive content to destabilize business activities.

Fortunately, they came up with several strict measures to control the situation and remove every security problem. Another rising problem that can lead to users' loss on the platform is the attack from cybercriminals on Zoom users. It can cause a significant backlash, and the platform can lose many users at the same time.

Links to China

There have been different accusations about selling data and information to another social media platform and reports linking the platform to the Chinese servers. Failing to come up with an excellent plan could be bad for customers. At some point in time, the chief executive officer at Zoom, Eric Yuan, made an admission of mistakenly routing calls through a server belonging to the Chinese to avoid network congestion. It is a rising problem for Americans using the platform because of its security problems.

Zoombombing/Zoom raiding

It is an unwanted intrusion by hackers into a video conference.

Zoom was initially planned to be utilized in business settings, where most people attempt their best to act professionally. That is why it's extremely significant for the teachers/host to know the best settings and highlights to use to help learn and limit disturbance.

Lightning Source UK Ltd.
Milton Keynes UK
UKHW052129281220
376007UK00001B/18

9 781801 546713